August 9, 2009

Danielle,

First off, Welcome to my family!
This book is to be used as a guide
to remind you what Kevin's Duties are,
now that he is your husband.
I am happy and proud of you both.
I hope this book serves you well.
Congrats!!

Love,
Shannon

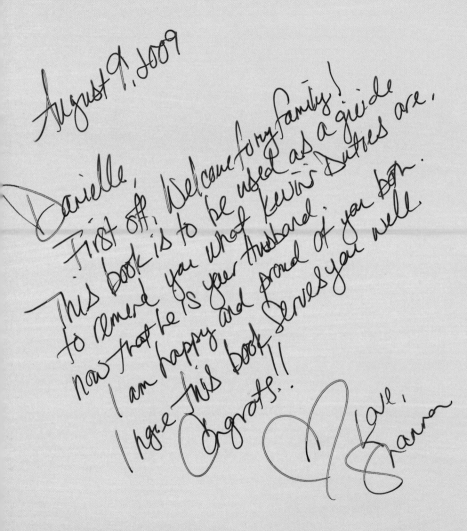

For Judy,
who knows a few more uses.
—T.M.

Library of Congress Cataloging-in-Publication Data Available

2 4 6 8 10 9 7 5 3 1

Published by Sterling Publishing Co., Inc.
387 Park Avenue South, New York, NY 10016

Distributed in Canada by Sterling Publishing
c/o Canadian Manda Group, 165 Dufferin Street
Toronto, Ontario, Canada M6K 3H6
Distributed in Great Britain by Chrysalis Books Group PLC
The Chrysalis Building, Bramley Road, London W10 6SP, England
Distributed in Australia by Capricorn Link (Australia) Pty. Ltd.
P.O. Box 704, Windsor, NSW 2756, Australia

Printed in China

Sterling ISBN 1-4027-2669-4

For information about custom editions, special sales, premium and
corporate purchases, please contact Sterling Special Sales
Department at 800-805-5489 or specialsales@sterlingpub.com.

38 Uses for a HUSBAND

Harriet Ziefert

drawings by
Todd McKie

Sterling Publishing Co., Inc.
New York

1.

diva

2.
grill master

3.
interior designer

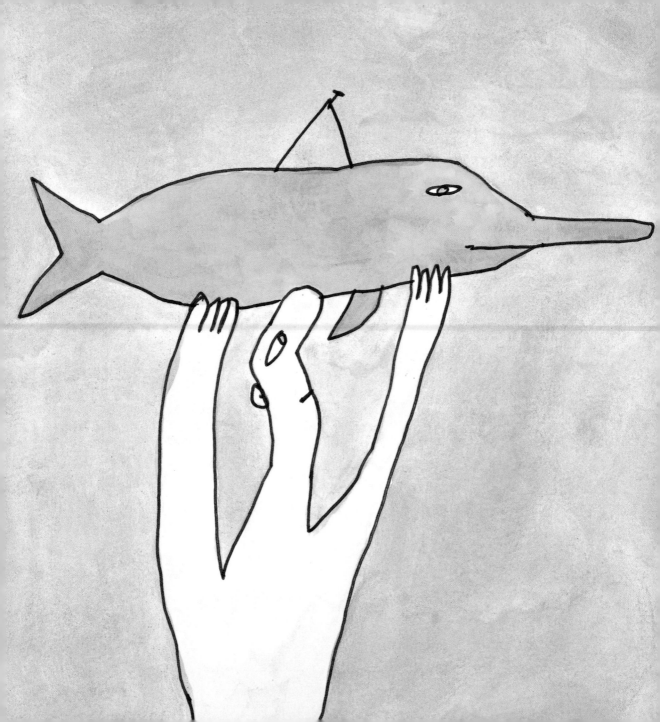

4.

object of desire

5.

climate control

6.

back scratcher

7.

loan officer

8.
IT specialist

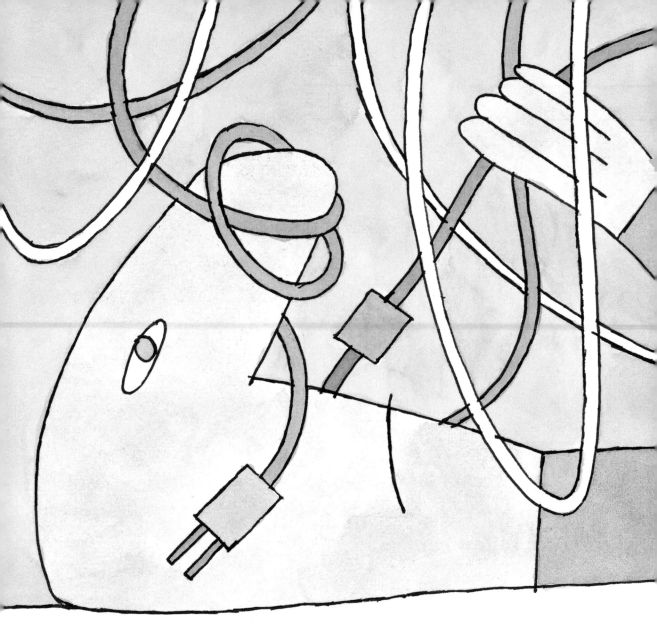

9.

mix master

10.

jar opener

11.

groundskeeper

12.
colorist

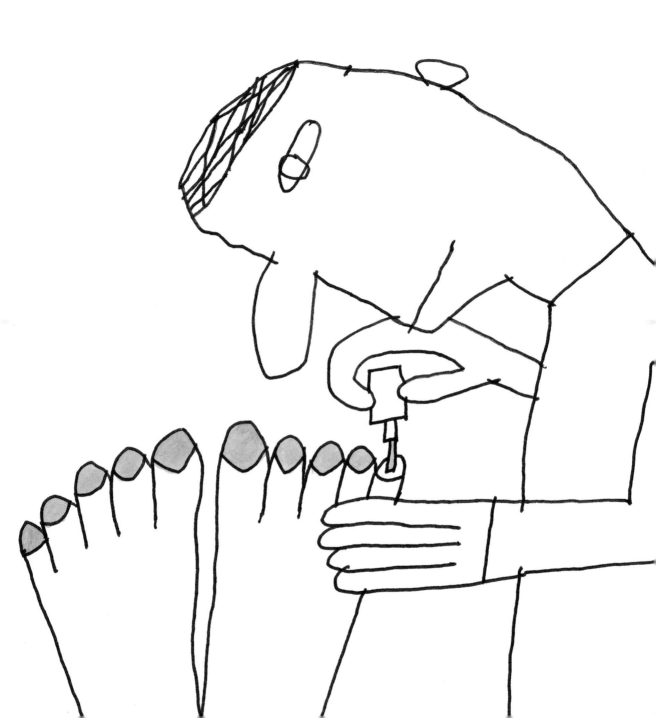

13.

partner

14.

nurse

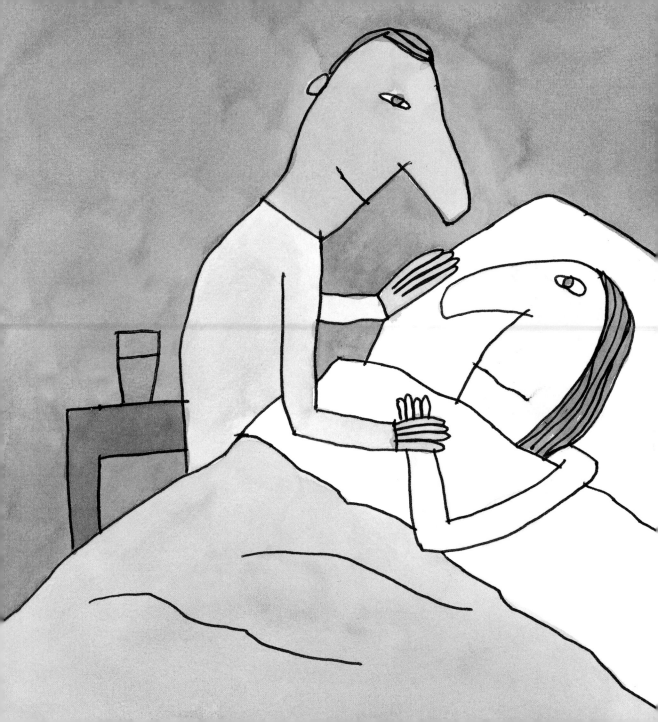

15.

pest control

16.
provider

17.

sous chef

18.

dance partner

19.

class clown

20.
giver of gifts

21.
back support

22.
baggage handler

23.

sommelier

24.

laundress

25.

plumber

26.

tree surgeon

27.
alchemist

28.
timekeeper

29.
worm handler

30.

gourmand

31.

obedience trainer

32.

emotional support

33.

horticulturist

34.
electrician

35.

zoo keeper

36.

connoisseur

37.
shelter

38.

companion